RUMOURS OF HOME

RUMOURS OF HOME

HIRO BOGA

DEVA PUBLISHING
UNITED KINGDOM • 2022

Copyright 2022 by Hiro Boga. All rights reserved. No part of this publication may be reproduced, stored in a retrieval system, or transmitted in any form or by any means, without prior written permission of the publisher, except by a reviewer who may quote brief passages in a review to be printed, broadcast, or published online.

Published by
Deva Publishing
Sunrising, Restronguet Weir, Falmouth, TR11 5SS United Kingdom

For

Jesse and James

home and belonging

*You are a current in the river
of Divine Flow*

*Love created you
Grace sculpted your face
in gold*

*You cannot earn your place here
You belong—*

*With every breath
you belong*

TABLE OF CONTENTS

STARSEEDS

We are the flying sparks	3
Joy climbs barefoot	4
When fear comes knocking	5
Make a cocoon of your heart	6
The turning leaf remembers spring	7
No ocean without a shore	8
What you nurture grows	9
To pursue perfection is to nail	10
In the clear air of this new day	11
The receding tide gathers up her silver skirts	12
You've pursued this dream for a long while	13
When I was a girl my heart leaped out	14
In this time of holy tenderness	15
Love is the underground stream	16
From first breath to last	17
Today, inhabit the epic chronology of a tree	18
To transform the world	19
You glimpse her galloping on the far horizon	20
In a singular embrace Wholeness cradles	21
What is yearning to be born?	22
As the chill of winter desiccates your bones	23
Upside down	24
Light blooms on the cold, calm sea	25
Does the rock demand of the river	26
The Love that fills your world with beauty	27
From the harbour of Kindness the boat of your heart	28

THE SCRIBBLED EMBROIDERY OF BIRDS

You are a Miracle	31
Redbird	34
When It's Freezing in February	35
When You Come to the End of the Path	37
Wild	39
Hunger	40
Tide Line	41
Dancing with Resistance	42
Until that Day	44
Last Night the Full Moon Shone a Slanting Light	45
Stand in Wonder at the Horizon's Open Door	46
Gather Starlight in the Shape of You	47
What You Know Now	48
Tug Power	51
Flight to Freedom	52
Fingerpainting	54
Duet	56
Post Mortem	57
The Things That Scare You	59
Roots	61
Wings	62
In the Country of the Heart	63
Show Me	64
No	65
Yes	67
No. Yes.	68
Hestia	69
You Opened Your Mouth	70
Kali	71
Anyway	72

Death Doesn't Hover	74
Winter Light	75
'Tis the Season of Sweet Dispersal.	76
Bird Girl	77
How To Fill the Hole Left by Banishing Your Soul	78
Lopsided Moon in the Jaws of Perfection	80
Round	82
Between Shelter and Flight	84

RUMOURS OF HOME

Serenade	86
Elegy	87
A Capella	88
Prayer	89
Invocation	90
Vocalises	92
Meditations From the Center	96
Tenaramente	104
The Feast of St. Thomas	106
Bodh Gaya	111
Buddhist Chronicles	113
Yasodhara & Siddhartha: The Parting	113
Rejection	115
Rahula's demand	116
Prajapati	117
Yasodhara's Lament	120
Suddodhana's Dilemma	121
Siddhartha at the Boundary of the Sakya Kingdom	122
At the Boundary: the River Anoma	123
Yasodhara	124
You	125
Peace Rises	126

STARSEEDS

We are the flying sparks
of stars and galaxies

Our bones articulate
the songs of constellations

Everything answers the call
to home

Every atom journeys
to the music of its belonging

Joy climbs barefoot
in her nightgown

turning on stars
in her star tree

When fear comes knocking
open the door

invite him in for tea
kiss his trembling cheek

Wholeness is the gift
at every threshold

Every visitor
is sacred

Make a cocoon of your heart

liquefy the bones
    of habit, identity
circumstance

    all the preening, pining selves

become unrecognizable

ride the wind
    into winged sky

the turning leaf
remembers spring

sorrow deeply felt
exhales joy

hummingbird's fragile wings
its glory

perfect vulnerability
is perfect strength

being yourself
is your gift

No ocean
without a shore

A river is a negotiation
between flow and riverbank

Blood needs arteries to carry it
from heart to limb

Love the sturdy shape
that holds your fluid self

What you nurture
grows

Nourish your freedom.
Feed your soul

Make your life
your art

Be yourself
O magnificent You!

To pursue perfection is to
    nail the scribbled embroidery of

birds in flight to a stone wall—
    something flinty, unyielding

utterly unlike the caressing air
    that bends to the beat of wings

The price for this pursuit is
    eternal vigilance
        a strict and joyless scrutiny

The tender heart grieves, its
    weaving, wavering flight denied

In the clear air of this new day
    may the bell of your heart

ring out your own perfect note

May your radiance be the sun
    enlivening your world

May your every breath be
    boundless blessing

May Love be your source,
    your gift, your unfolding story

Peace be with you. Infinite peace

The receding tide gathers up
    her silver skirts

flees to the bladed moon—
    home of her first longing.

Alone in that celestial void
    she falters, turns

stumbles home to the warm
    shore of her belonging

You've pursued this dream
for a long while

caught glimpses of her white heels
disappearing around corners.

Finally, you arrive at the edge of
the woods where she waits.

You're dishevelled, out of breath
a little afraid.

She smiles, turning to you
your own beloved, unfamiliar face.

When I was a girl
my heart leaped out to the
star-salted sky, where I belonged

Now, I grow into this patient shore
a sea-smoothed pebble
at home in fertile ground

In this time of holy tenderness
feel the seed of your Self sunk deep
in the loamy dark

where the husk of who you've been
shelters your becoming

Soon, light's fingers will shred
the hood that holds
your greening glory

Love is the
underground stream

that greens
the fallow world

The naked heart opens
a tremulous wound

to Love's patient
irrigation

From first breath
to last

you become
the song you sing

Who
are you becoming?

Today
inhabit the epic chronology
of a tree

In a thousand years
your life will be
rich humus on forest floor

shelter
of a forest canopy

To transform the world
choose love
choose to be kind

choose
clear-voiced truth

choose the complexities of wholeness—
do it today

Every choice
becomes the world

You glimpse her galloping
on the far horizon

the spirit of Adventure
riding bareback

wind lifting her heels
summoning the sun

soul sister, heart's wild
twin, another
    you

In a singular embrace
Wholeness cradles:

Love's pregnant arrival
the iniquities of loss

sweet water and salt
the keening of galaxies

stars that pulse
in the belly of the Earth

and you
    undeniable you

What is yearning
to be born?

What is feathering back
into light?

Between farewell and welcome
the bridge of your heart

As the chill of winter desiccates
your bones, ask yourself:

what is cold, huddled, banished
within you?

Will you love it back
to the pulse of life

bring it home to the hearth
of your heart?

What happens when you open
your arms, say Welcome! Welcome!

Upside down
inside out

Grace transforms you

Light blooms on the cold, calm sea
in whose depths the shattered bones of hope
knit a new wholeness

Does the rock demand of the river:
Flow North! I want to play
with polar bears!

Does the river change course
to meet the rock's desire?

If you are a river
flow to the sea!

If you are a rock, kneel
on the river bed.

The Love that fills your world with beauty
your lungs with air
provides everything you need

Everything

Nothing that is truly yours
can be lost, stolen
or taken away

Knowing that you cannot lose
you are free to create, free to choose

From the harbour of
    Kindness

      the boat of your heart
        sets sail

            for the blurred horizon

Be kind, sweet traveller
      We are all

      finding our way
            home

THE SCRIBBLED EMBROIDERY OF BIRDS

YOU ARE A MIRACLE

You are beautiful!

So beautiful, I could sit and gaze at you all day
and drown in wonder
as night falls and Time dissolves.

You are magnificent.

You hold the sky as lightly as a bubble
in the palm of your hand.

You, my friend, are the light that shines through the tender green of this leaf
and brings eternity into focus.

You are the restless power of the sea
and the yielding boundary of the shore.

You are the freedom of wild geese
on the far horizon.

You turn your elegant head
and the Earth spins on her axis

You are all that is Necessary
and Sufficient.

You dream the stars from their home in the belly of the Earth.

Your circle of inner selves is the crown that shelters,
the lap that cradles.

The bead of sweat on your fingertip
nourishes the whole, hungry world.

What will you do, with all this power?

Who will you be, when you see your true reflection?

Come, visit the Pool of Remembering with me.
Even a puddle will do.

Come, see your true reflection.

Everything conspires to show you your Self.
Everything conspires to make you visible.

Will you rise on the horizon
in the Land of Wagging Fingers?

Will you become a Pool of Remembering
for them too?

Write the truth of your being on your body.
With your naked finger, write...

I am beautiful!

I am magnificent!

I am you!

And you!

And you!

Write it! Sing it! Say it!

I am love.

We are love.

Our business —
O, our business is love.

REDBIRD

Redbird sails between wind-ploughed
clouds, trailing sparks through
rumbling sky.

His watchful eye droops on a single
silky stalk
reflects humming mountains
ruffled seas
a small boy adrift on a river of moonlight.

He saw me, Redbird
winked his one blue eye
solemn as a sphinx
sailing past on crimson wings
gliding a green current
swift as the shiver of birch trees.

He tossed a mottled feather
in my open mouth—
not a promise, an
invitation
from the riotous watermelon horizon.

WHEN IT'S FREEZING IN FEBRUARY

When it's freezing in February
February and freezing

I'll slip into my story quilt and dream.

> *emerald droplets fly into the night
> from the cup of my hands in your cold,
> swift waters. sky widens the arc of your
> unknown*

When it's freezing in February
in February, freezing

my story slips quilted into dreams.

> *The sky has its own gravity. Fire-flies
> streak like songs into the night; the eyes
> of shooting stars.*

When it's freezing in February

and February is freezing

    my quilt slips dreaming into story.

        who are you?
        naked
            orphan?
      egg

    watch the lines on your palms
        shift, woman, like sand on this river bed

    the moon bends to listen
to the hush

      begin

When it's February, February, freezing, February
story, quilt, dream.

WHEN YOU COME TO THE END OF THE PATH

When you come to the end of the path
it isn't obvious.

There are openings under the trees
where small streams have carved what looks like

a way forward.

The forest floor is golden with fallen fir needles
and at first you think Ah yes! Here's a trail

or at least a deer path to follow.

A half-hour later, maybe more, you find yourself
lost. The same heavy-boned trees all around

the same openings that lead nowhere.

The drip drip drip of drooping branches. Weird creaks
and groans, echoes without direction.

You lean against a slick black rock, slippery with mosses
clusters of emerald stars in no visible constellation.

You're not afraid, exactly. After all, there are paths
through these woods. You've walked them before

on Sunday afternoons much like this one. You have
a nodding acquaintance with several spectacular ferns

and at least one flaming arbutus tree whose scarlet trunk
you pat fondly whenever you pass by.

Now, you sniff the air the way you've seen dogs do —
that keen alertness, that panting relationship with geography.

Maybe you'll don a dog's intelligence when you assume
its stance — the hidden pattern of the woods revealed

in your canine nose.

The trees stand, inscrutable, silent. No sun-dappled path
appears magically before you, inviting your foot

to its ordained destination.

You're hungry, now. You're cold. The light
thins overhead.

You lean your heart into the slanting rain
and walk.

WILD

**Wild is anything that's not at home
in something else's place...**
– *Wendell Berry*

Today, this wind my home
                              Today
                   this lucid sky

Today, I own nothing—
am owed
nothing. Today

    only

          throatsong, eyesong
          brimming
wind, lucid sky

today

          no name, no face, no
            story

today

      wild—

wild

HUNGER

You and I are begging bowls waiting
to be filled

our needs much simpler
than we believe them to be.

The bell of our tongues knows nothing

of the shrunken belly's hunger
for infinity

TIDE LINE

Yesterday, I walked the tide line
on the beach below my house.

In wet sand, black pebbles embedded
echo receding waves

The activity of tide made visible.

That's what our lives are—
the activity of the Sacred

made visible—
one pattern receding, as the next one arrives.

DANCING WITH RESISTANCE

is a slow waltz with a great gorilla. Hot, scratchy.
A sweaty, fumbling dance that tastes like copper
pennies. That exhales a bitter breath.

> *I cannot see.*
> *His shoulders fill the world, and I cannot see.*

Those long arms hold me firmly to a chest
as unyielding as my grandmother's—
a great acreage of fur that blinds me.

He dances me backward, *quick-quick*
sl-o-w, a ship's prow parting the swirling sea
and we sail off the dance floor, sail out

of the room, lumber into shadows, into a
jasmine-scented garden, loud with crickets
and the soft croaking

of frogs. He pushes me down with his great
hairy chest onto a wooden bench. His massive head
trembles—he looks as though he might weep.

A river of stars spills across the sky.

He wraps a violet shawl around my bare shoulders.
Pats my back, grunts, sniffs the air for danger.
Throws back his head and howls

howls his animal grief.

UNTIL THAT DAY

When I die, I want to be this log—
a nursery for green and growing things.

Small trees spring from my body—
shy, exuberant, leaping towards sunshine.

This must be how the Earth feels
about people, grasses, whales—

all of us green and growing,
rooted in her belly.

Until that day, that final fall
I'll practice being the Earth.

LAST NIGHT THE FULL MOON SHONE A SLANTING LIGHT

Last night the full moon shone a slanting light
across my winter garden
where two deer lay sleeping

under the leafless apple tree
whose arthritic arms beamed wands of light
through the twitching caverns
of their dreams

while I, too restless to dream
climbed the vanilla mast of my bed
and sailed out to the curved elbow

of the far horizon whose There
hauled me home
without apology

STAND IN WONDER AT THE HORIZON'S OPEN DOOR

Feel the threshold's rough grain
beneath your feet.

Do not turn around. Do not listen to the
beseeching voices, the fearful voices
calling you back to what you've known.

You belong to the future now. Go. Find
wet grass, sharp shale, silken sand
to hold you.

You are in the embrace of That
which moves you.

You are That. You are That.

GATHER STARLIGHT IN THE SHAPE OF YOU

Ride your radiance
through the rivers of the universe

You are light
and the source of light

Bring your luminosity
to the feast of constellations

WHAT YOU KNOW NOW

1.

Empty of sight you gave yourself away
to those

who were blind to your gift
as you were. You.

They devoured your sweet juices,
spit out the pith and rind of you

as you did. You.

2.

Years went by. Watchful, rind-thick, rind-bitter,
you cradled the memory of your treasure

buried it
in a mountain cave

guarded by the stench of dragon breath.

You did. You.

3.

Your sweet citrus selves, deprived
of light, of air

shriveled, curled their pithy threads
around your dwindling heart.

In your dank cave, you dreamed of orange groves—
the sun-drenched country of your becoming.

4.

Now, on this dappled mountainside
you've built your home.

Windows open wide to a curved horizon.
Skylights, for visiting stars and spilled constellations.

A floor and walls of hand-rubbed stone.
You made this. You.

5.

Strangers sometimes climb the rocky path
to your front door.

You welcome them with cool water,
oranges in a blue clay bowl.

You do not give yourself away.
You do not withhold.

6.

You know this, now. You were always yours to give.

Yours, and more than yours —

to take, to bury
to hold, nourish, offer, radiate.

TUG POWER

This.

This log boom gliding silently
on pewter waves
tethered umbilical to a single
tug.

Squat, snub-nosed, face only a mother
could love—
this small bundle of muscle
and will

pulls a once-upon-a-time forest effortlessly—
a loggy wake.

O, the power of purposeful alignment!

The power of faithful service
hauling a forest

home.

FLIGHT TO FREEDOM

My ancestors launched into the Arabian Sea
in tiny coracles fragile as leaves
to escape the *jihad*.

Their country
torched by Arab invaders, their people
slaughtered in the name of Allah

they entrusted their bodies to the tides,
sailed east to India; fled
for their lives and for freedom to worship

Ahura Mazda, the god
of their ancestors. The year
was 760 AD.

Thirteen hundred years later, I took flight
westward across that churning sea.
Seeds of their spirit

in me. Those ancestors,
with their wandering blood, keep me questing,
peregrine.

I do not own the comforts
of their religion, seek instead a god

who lives in me; am impelled
not by raiders but
by this spirit's urgent embarkation

to be free.

FINGER PAINTING

Sea foam sparkles on the waves. Sea lions
roar. Foam shivers, flies
into the wind. The tide holds its breath.
Hisssssssssssss

———

Ganesh's belly rests in his lap. His trunk
caresses tree, root, sky. His feet can't be so
small, can they? To hold up such a big heart?

———

Black grapes in a white bowl. Thick skin, sweet
wetness on the tongue.

———

Giraffes nibble lilac clouds.
One gulp. All gone.

Follow this dimpled eddy down down *down*. Blue-green
sea green, azure, mink. Murky mists. Sun
shines up from its sea bed. Stars shatter across the sky.

From the beach below, a springy rainbow path
sends a formal invitation. Walk on water. Walk on air. Walk
through the stars. Walk ... walk ... walk ... out
to the edge ... in
to home.

Yesterday, you were a tired old man. Today, you're
three-and-a-half. Today, you rule the world.
One flick of your pigtails and ... off with their heads!

Roses. Spicy-musk. Hidden under the floor-boards. Exuding
rose-ness, a tang of cloves.

Tomorrow, a whisper curls around every ear.
Have you heard? The tide is here!

DUET

Heart's small voice sings

we

    us

        this

            yes!

Heart wears itself on its own sleeve; it delights in slippery mud and fallen petals. It kisses Head's myriad gray pleats and great, furrowed brow. Head mutters: *you*

> *time-waster, mooner, you singer who can't reach high c; mistake-maker, incontinent bleeder; giver of gifts you cannot afford; blissed-out, undiscriminating, lacerated fool*

Yes! sings heart

bird

    flower

        rock

           fish

                star

starfishrockbirdflower!

POST MORTEM

This is my father's child, Mother. My
half-sister, Marguerite, here
in this photograph. I know you are angry,
but bonds of blood compelled me here.
I had to see her; could not will her
into non-existence, as you do.

She should have been at Papa's funeral,
she had the right. You would not allow it.
I understand. He had another
family, one we knew nothing
about, secreted in the snowy scrub
of central Saskatchewan. These are facts.

She is thirteen. Those trips —
to Ottawa, Papa said — returning somber,
silent, grief scoring his back, the night
the telephone rang and you answered,
but no-one replied.

You are angry. So am I. Did we
know this man? And yet. She has his clear
grey eyes, that stolid wedge of chin, scimitar
nose, sudden smile. He phoned her, the afternoon
before he died, told her he loved her.

Never once told me. In twenty years, not
once, Mother, although I knew.
Such reticence left him lonely, a
planet orbiting a distant
sun, our silences a language, the body's

mute offering. But here, in these horizontal
plains he was transformed, a man who told
his daughter she was the rain that greened

the parched and fallow fields
of his heart.

THE THINGS THAT SCARE YOU

Make a great circle
A hundred feet around.

Drop in it all the things
that scare you.

Fly into the air
five hundred feet

a thousand feet.
Higher—ten thousand feet.

Ten thousand feet.

E x p a n d to fill the sky.

Look down at your circle.

How does the center shape
the boundary?

See the things that scare you
held safely

in the circle's embrace.

See the boundary
become the center.

Goblins and ghosts flow back
in time

become children, toddlers, beloved
babies.

Return, fly home
with the sun in your wings.

ROOTS

All you yearn for is held in trust
for you.

Press the soles of your feet
into this loamy earth, drink

from underground tributaries.

Go in and down, not out
and up. Spirit

is not separation. You are sacred—
your body

the heartwood of the greening tree.

We are tree and root and earth
entwined, unfurling.

WINGS

On the balcony of our house in Bombay,
my mother grew dragons in pots. Their
shimmering heads emerged from dark soil,
wobbled on delicate necks, grew muscular,
breathed gusts of fire. Their scales were iridescent,
light shimmered in peacock folds on their backs.

Eventually, they smashed the pots with their tails,
their leathery wings opened and they flew
around the house, hovered above the balcony,
settled on the terrace. At night they slept
under my bed. One dragon had a tongue
of silver. One breathed gold. One scorched my
eyebrows when he laughed. One bit a hole

in my heart, planted a dragon seed, which
grew and grew. Now a baby dragon flicks
its tail between my shoulder-blades, between
the shadow and its whisper:

wings, wings

IN THE COUNTRY OF THE HEART

In the country of the heart the baby rabbit sleeps
shaded by Eagle's wings
sheltered from noonday sun

Fierce and tender held
in the same thudding heartbeat
the pulse that carries, the beat that rides

Surging sea and star-flung sky
silent budding earth
firebright, starbright, spilled-ink moon

  Listen

The world leans to your whisper

  Listen

The wind releases its cry

 Listen

The Beloved's breath in your ear

  Shhhhhh ... listen

SHOW ME

Show me in your emerald heart, in the
current of your river. Show me how
to open my hands, your laughing light
trembling between my palms

    Beloved, show me

I have left the house with no roof. Hands ache
from clutching water, gripping air. No
ground, no walls, no rooms. I have left them all

behind. See my boat leak. See the boatman
return to our ruined village. My clothes
left on the river bank. I don't know how

to swim, how

    I have forgotten my name

NO

I say no to plunder and papayas
ripped from their beds at midnight, the black pearls
of their seeds crushed under careless feet. no

to raids on houses of the poor who must
lick their honey off the edge of a razor
blade. no to revenge; no to seductions

that ring like crystal goblets stained ruby-red
with the wine of entitlement. I bite
the hand that reaches for cream without passing
the coffee. I say no

to arguments about angels dancing
on the heads of pins. angels have better
things to do — tend to plants and babies

mothers and turtles, those who stay home
move slowly, live close to the ground. who do
not expect the universe to throw them

a meteor shower to celebrate every
changed diaper or the patient laying
and hatching of eggs. I say no to clutched

fists and fires that feed on stolen fuel. no
to being buried in the Department
of Home Furnishings at Sears. no.

no.

YES

now this is what I feed myself: sleep
in the nest of my feather bed; buttered
cream of wheat with goat's milk and cardamom

beethoven quartets, shimmering jazz
renata tebaldi's legs wrapped around
verdi. poems that bloom like roadside daisies

jane hirshfield, seamus heaney
basho. rumi
white chrysanthemums in a blue vase

my fingers like warm wax around the barrel
of this pen; lined paper beaded with the
mercury of my heart. the peace of things

their comfort, silently offered, their patient
giving. round plates with red and yellow rims
cobalt cups, hot as the kiln which fired them

the perfect heft of stainless steel forks
shallow ponds of spoons. the beauty — the
sturdy, honest beauty of things, ungelded

by tricks of light on water, innocent
of tidal undertow

NO. YES.

What gives you the right to grab what is not yours
to take? You have grown large on piracy,
swollen like a balloon on breath stolen
from children who no longer sleep or fill
their lungs because you have convinced them the
air belongs to you; their breath, their dreams
belong to you. You have taken the tender
bamboo of their hearts and boiled it into
broth to nourish you, Appetite.
You have sucked the marrow from their bones and
grinned with relish at the brine of blood on your
tongue. Your *table d'hote* is not unique. Genghis
Khan fed at it, made menus of the lives
of those who loved him; cast around for more—
always more—to fill a hole as cavernous
as you.

No

———

Every no bears in its belly the sibilant
yes: a pomegranate seed white in its
sheath of translucent red

HESTIA

You gods and bearded prophets, go squabble
in the pub for a while. I've heard enough
of heroes and lightning chariots streaking
across the sky. My companions are Cassandra
and Cordelia. They cook with me and wash
dishes afterwards. This chipped blue bowl
into which I dip my spoon is the
goddess's face. The hand, which caresses —
its tendons and veins and miraculous
fingers — works her threads of light into
muscular days.

I kneel to scrub the floor.

YOU OPENED YOUR MOUTH

You opened your mouth and swallowed it all
believing purity of heart could transform
mercury into mead by some
mysterious alchemy of the spirit.

You sucked in poisoned milk; you swallowed stones
disguised as potato soup. Bullets rumbled
in your belly, which grew round as the full
moon stuffed with shattered rabbit bones.

Heart without wisdom is a blind woman
boiling lentils in acid rain.

KALI

Kali, queen of the night-sky, your skull
necklace rattles on dancing breasts.
Blood stains the cavern and corners
of your mouth. Your obsidian face gleams;
your ruby tongue defies all who claim dominion.
Your many hands grip many lethal weapons —
swift swords and whirling discus; lightning
cracks open this labyrinthine brain, its convoluted
folds sizzle into mist. Silence returns
to the sky, to the heart.

Around a demon's hair, your hennaed hands
are curled; his severed head swings above
the earth; ragged droplets drip scarlet from his
neck's stump. Broad, black feet — your feet — stamp
on his headless body; your eyes are fierce
coal-stars, every eyelash a cluster of
constellations. Such power, milady, I
am breathless at this naked red display —
my own long shrouded in seemly white.

I'll strip off these penitent robes, unpin
my hair, let it float above my roaring
chest. And shout, a bawdy barker bellowing:
come, take — enter if you dare!

ANYWAY

When your smile is razor wire.
Your apology, a blade.
When your impunity is a boot
on a vulnerable neck.

When your horizon shrivels with your point of view.
When what you believe you are owed
smashes through flesh and bone
showering you in stolen blood.

Earth cradles you in her lap
anyway.
Sun shines on you
anyway.
The world spills her beauty at your feet
anyway.

Your heart a stone.
Your mind a trip-wire.
Belly boiling with unappeasable greed.
Eyes blind to the miracle of light.

You are the beloved of the earth anyway.

You are beloved anyway.

DEATH DOESN'T HOVER

stinking up the room with sweaty feet.

She is velvet-soft, night-sky radiant.

In her arms I melt, astonished.
Unclench my fists,
Expand, expand into her embrace.

She smells of night-blooming jasmine.

She stands at her threshold,
opens wide her front door, welcomes me in,

Come, sit, visit—
rest awhile, she says.
It's not your time to live here,
but you can visit anytime you want.

Heart unfurled,
I am home here, as I am home
in my own bed.

Stars crackle in her hearth.
The world breathes through her window.

WINTER LIGHT

Through November's grey flannel,
leafless trees open their branches to
light's airy passage between trunk and twig.

Rhodo's leaves tent downward in the mist
brave buds yearning at their peaks,
trembling in cold wind, drinking light.

For many years now, Winter and I have not
been friends. This year, I meet it gladly.
Old friend, silvered like me, bare-branched

like me. Wind-woven, mist soft, I know you
in my skin, in winter rain that rivers
through my limbs. I know your grace—

your generous, mouldering, mulching grace
sheltering seeds, nurturing a future
you will not live to see.

'TIS THE SEASON OF SWEET DISPERSAL.

Leaves adrift on beds of smoke,
on tourniquets of ash. Sky bleached
by fire's furious labour.

Let us be done with the violence
of accumulation.

May what remains bless us as it flies past
trailing songs of freedom
flinging wide the cloak of containment.

BIRD GIRL

There's a blackbird in her bones
who flaps and flaps and flaps
her wings, desperate
for flight into that empyrean blue,
her natural element, only now

it's not.

She can't get lift-off
and anytime she tries too hard—
that fourth flap!—she falls
belly to ground, finally, finally learning
the humble art of being human.

HOW TO FILL THE HOLE LEFT BY BANISHING YOUR SOUL

eat things. fatty, salty, sweet things
obsess about eating — green juice! organic kale! vegan! raw!

buy things: big things — cars, houses, yachts, planes,
sentient beings, entire countries
luxury trips to remote pacific islands,
haute couture, ethically sourced diamonds
small things — shoes, hats, bags, furniture, clothes
living things — labradoodle, cat, chihuahua, python,
tree, star, sky
dead things — stuffed birds, stuffed animals, furs,
trophy fish, coral reefs

kill thing — honeybees, bats, whales
hunt the world's rarest species, for sport
denude the countryside of songbirds so you can eat the
tiniest bird carcass
start a revolution, or a terrorist cell —
kill everyone who's not exactly like you

kill things silently, under the radar—
decimate funding for babies and the poor
veterans, homeless, disenfranchised
bully to the brink of homicide
or induced suicide
pretend it was all a joke, or it never happened

know things
the price of everything; the value of nothing—
the encyclopedia brittanica, recited backwards, in gaelic
the bible, chapter and verse, as literal as lead

have opinions about everything, especially things
with which you are entirely unacquainted
destroy everyone who doesn't agree with you

hoard things
fears, doubts, insecurities
what-if, yes-but, no-never, yes-always
grudges, envy, hatred, rage

deny things
if you can't see it, it don't exist—nope!
i never!
who, me?
evolution? the devil's invention!
climate collapse? fake, fake news!

LOPSIDED MOON IN THE JAWS OF PERFECTION

She hangs like a crooked brooch in a perfect, sable sky. Your fingers itch to straighten her, just so—a little more to the left, a little higher in the upper right-hand corner. Yes.

But then, there's her disappointing light, that shade of curdled cream, so unlike the burnished yolk of her magnificent brother, Sun. Even the pale stars glimmer more elegantly, are more presentable than this disgrace of a moon.

Maybe she's best covered up. Where's that black silk shawl, the one that gleams like the night sky? The one you bought to wear to a certain artists' soiree, just last week? Quick! Pull it out of its tissue paper bed, hold it up against the window, veil that sickly moon.

Ugh ... wrong hue. It won't do.

Maybe you'll just close your eyes then, make that crooked moon, with her mottled grin, disappear. What's she got to grin about anyway? Can't hang straight, can't shine right! Shameless, revealing that naked face!

The world needs beauty, elegance, gorgeousness!
It's a spiritual imperative—everyone knows that.

You pull out your perfect black dress from your cedar-lined closet, slip it on with sky-high heels, a narrow belt that gleams like the sun. Style your hair just so, a parabolic arc sweeping down the curve of your cheek, framing those Mont-Blanc cheek bones.

An unflinching hour in front of the mirror and your hair won't do what it's supposed to. Your jaw is irredeemably jowly; Audrey Hepburn you're not. Lopsided. Like the moon with its brazen grin—tawdry as a trinket and just as out of place— hanging crookedly against that perfect, sable sky.

Abandoned mid-stroke, your painting breathes quietly in its dusty corner. Stranded on the shoals of a stuttering stanza, your poem blinks its transponder light through stormy dreams of perfection, navigating, navigating you home.

ROUND

She won't be held
in pants with tightly buttoned waists,
their tailored creases knifing into
glittering conversations. She won't enter
the clamorous avenues of your angular world.

Her roundness deflects your demands.
She will not offer you mirrored surfaces, the comfort
of your own high-powered reflection. She is mute
that way. She holds her counsel as she holds
the undulant hive that spins sunshine
in the moonlit chamber of her symmetry.

Her home is in the round hills. You must climb
a long way to reach her and then
the mouth of her cave is hidden in thickets of box thorn,
prickly pear, nettles, desert mallow.

You must want her enough to go looking for her.
Shed your city clothes, risk being stung
on the soles of your feet. You must be brave.

You call, call out.
Your voice echoes off the red hills, disappears
in the thin, sage-scented air.

You turn away. And then, perhaps,
you'll hear it—
a single thrumming note that builds, reverberates,
a stream of golden honey from a hundred thousand bees
pouring into the startle of your ear.

BETWEEN SHELTER AND FLIGHT

Today, all that shelters me descends
with the sudden, clamorous weight
of a collapsed safari tent. Tangled

in its heavy canvas, its guy wires and
flapping doorway, I struggle
to my knees, scrape the palm of my hand

against flinty ground, stagger upright
in the ruins of shelter gone rogue,
its domed roof and foldaway

walls revealed for what they are:
a flimsy intervention.

Until the bird in me, that
leather-winged pterodactyl,
resumes its interrupted flight

choosing the accommodation of wings
to uplifting air, leaving this pretext
of shelter far, far behind.

SERENADE

Feet planted in mud, cinnamon silt, sand
I rise to you through wavering green water.
Through blooms of algae, tangled weeds, I rise
unfold in the arbor of your tendrilled sun.
I rise, sweet breath of life, to you,

Breathe your fragrant air. Rooted
in tangles of despair I rise, sweet singer,
to your song, and all my yearning
yields to the height, breadth
and depth of you. I rise, great bard, to you.

And in that meeting-place of pond and sky
my I dissolves in your
boundless, boundless welcome.

ELEGY

When I bend and bind
squeeze my soul into narrow shoes,
deck it out in gaudy hues
of other people's clothing;
when I alter my inherent shape, strut
through attenuated alleyways of dialectic,
I lose you, crumble. I know
you are in me but I cannot reach you
in the rubble of my ignorance.

Such loneliness engulfs me
then, not all the soft-voiced friends, sultry
gongs of lust and wine assuage.
I am orphaned,
a lover bereft, a leather-shod beast without
breath, a vast homesick wail
in the wilderness.

I am homesick.

A CAPELLA

My life is bread-making.
Daily I work the dough.

My hands blend, shape it
into supple balls and then

I wait for your sacrament
of warm brown flour, sea-salt

water, a sprinkled
benediction

to expand in me
dissolving this mass

becoming
a fine leavening.

PRAYER

Let me embrace you
naked as rain.

Let all that is not me fall
away. This body, yielding to earth's
molten heart, this mind echoing
your fingerprint, these avid ears

drinking your elemental voice.
Let me know you in clamoring
cities, viridian hills
in curled fists of my sleeping child.

Let me embrace you
naked as rain.

INVOCATION

In this moment is the grace
of your presence. Yet as your star

brings daybright light
to the shadowed world, so your words
flow from my fingertips
onto this page —

veils across our union.

You are that which moves and is moved,
wind that sets reeds singing
and dancing, ancient reed beds
that murmur and sway.

You the sun's ardent kissing
the rushing river, you the river of leaping.

Birdsongs ring the vault of heaven —
hawk and horizon, wind and wing, all you.

You the limpid sky in whose bowl
clouds tumble. You the nimbostratus pall
that precipitates. Cedar tree and earth,

the seed from which the embryo grows—
the slow turnings of gestation, are you.

The Pleiades, Andromeda, the blazing
of your love. All worlds are you.

VOCALISES

1.

Break my heart open
with the hammer

of your love.

Grind me to powdered
sand. Blow me on *khamsins*

of your breath

into the deserts
of the world.

2.

The sun
comes

and smooths
my shadow

into silk.
You

sculpt
my reflection

in gold

3.

Burn

until my candle
melts

in tongues of flame

burn in me

4.

I come to you empty,
mind and heart hollow

Fill me
with the thrumming
of your presence

5.

My heart is fierce
longing. I am
the tumult of this world.
Bring me home. I lead to nothing
else. Where I go
you are.
No I, only
we, only all.

6.

Let me love you
as silence loves the seed of sound

as you love me

Let me love
as salt spray loves the seasoned shore

as you love

Let me
as all is you

be you.

MEDITATIONS FROM THE CENTER

bones glow
under lucent membrane

and the pulse, and the pulse

the pulse, Beloved,
    is you

In the center of my heart, a generous sun
in whose radiance
apple trees bloom

In the center of my heart, a chamber
through which the mistrals of heaven blow

In the center of my heart
songbirds till a garden

In the center of my heart, a round
window through which a meadowlark
flies out

In the center of my heart a living
pearl illumines the stars

In the center of my heart emerald mountains
ring a sapphire lake

In the center of my head is a rain-washed
dawn

In the center of my head cirrus clouds race
across cobalt sky

In the center of my head a hermit thrush
sings sweet wilderness

In the center of my head a bare room
opens in the fragrance of your hands

In the center of my head a mirror
your face reflected

In the centre of my head, wet sand
bears the footprints of our love

In the center of my crown an ocean laughs

In the center of my crown a heron
skims the blue rim of Earth

In the center of my crown
a cloud-wreathed peak
pierces your skin

In the center of my crown is a
wooden ladder you climb
down to meet me
and I
climb up to meet you

In the center of our crown, an orbit
of grace

a meadow of wildflowers
in which we lie down crushing wood-violets

blue, blue fragrance in the center
of my crown

In the center of my throat is templed
silence

the Great Void rings in the center of my throat

boats skim the sea on wind-whipped sails
sing you in the center of my throat

underground river-run
red-rock canyon roar

in the center in the center
center of my throat

whispering clanging amorous bells
in the center, in the center

center of my throat

In the center of my ribs, a silver salmon
leaps

In the center of my ribs, a star-tree shivers
from roots to sky

In the shelter of an oak a red-winged
blackbird
nests

In a viridian
pond, mallards teach
their ducklings to swim

In the center of my ribs, an infant
breathes

an angel
with hair of green willow
in the center of my ribs

In the center of my belly a red arbutus
overleaps the edge of a cliff

In the center of my belly a healing rain
widens the channels of a river
flowing into the sea

dolphins dream and play
in the center of my belly

a net of stars flies across ink-dark trees
in the center
in the center of my belly

In the center of my womb a resinous tree
fragrant sandalwood
branches

an angel of humor trades stories
with wide-eyed children

In the center of my womb a tribe of dancers
twirls the ribbon of the world

In the center of my womb a red-rock wilderness
whose name only you and I know

trails of starlight
big-bellied moon
in the center of my womb

TENARAMENTE

I stand at the boundary. On this side, familiar terrain. Hills like lyric waves brushed with sage, dew an aria on my tongue, golden wedge of light on my elbow. My arms know precisely my baby's milky weight, his warm mouth loose against my breast, my nipple cooling in this lambent dawn. Moss fur nuzzles the soles of my feet.

This is the threshold: this granite arch soaring skyward in the middle of a mustard field, keystone lost in the limpid blue of heaven. Ahead, unknown country. Images pour through my head like rain: Death in rusty black cloak, hooded, faceless, scythe gripped in blanched fingers. And bodies, light as dried laurel leaves, borne on bamboo biers, covered in marigolds; tinkling cymbals, heartbeat of drums, chanting voices bearing the soul back home.

That which is before me is veiled in light. My hand through the archway no longer a hand, effulgence of ultraviolet pulsing to a rhythm familiar as my heartbeat, enigmatic as an atom. I lean my upper body through the arch. Soft. Smell of almond blossoms, sticky fig-juice, olive groves. Shiver of argent sound, bells, chiming inside and out into one, my skin no longer my skin, no boundary, but a dissolved definition. An exchange of electrons and protons with ambient life which once bore many names — tree, fish, star, mud. My flesh and theirs transmuted into vibration, dance of particles into waves, waves and particles, call and answer, calando, dolce, dolce, tranquillo. I am a sympathetic string in a great aeolian harp, vibrating to the melody of these rushing winds, vast ripples of light and air and spirit.

Step now across the slate-gray stones. Prelude over, my voice flows into this canon which sings the Real. My infant son plays in the crack between worlds, time in his right hand, eternity in his left. He puts God in his mouth and savors, rolling divinity on his tongue, face rapt, chortling his own cantata.

THE FEAST OF ST. THOMAS

Love your brother as your soul; guard him as the pupil of your eye.

– *The Gospel of Thomas*

They come from far and wide, these men and women,
carrying babies on their hips,
solemn in their Sunday best.
Scraggly lines of them shuffle along
to view my body in this open coffin where it has lain,
unblemished and immaculately preserved,
for two thousand years. That miracle
so impressed the pope, he proclaimed me a saint.
So they come, these fishermen and shopkeepers
housewives, grandmothers, murmuring
prayers, entreaties, bargaining with God.
Their prayers rise up to heaven, as smoke.

The air in this church is thick with incense, yellow
with the light of sulphurous candles lit
by these pilgrims for the souls of their dead.

    Love your brother as your soul ...

The Syrian Bishop of Kerala raises his arms
in blessing; purple robes and snowy miter proclaim

his holy office. Thousands kneel to kiss his ring before
bending to kiss the feet of the body I left behind
so many centuries ago. Hundreds faint, unable to breathe
the close and humid air in St. Thomas's cathedral.

Imagine! They named a cathedral after me.
After me, Thomas, who never knew
where I'd rest my head at night
once I entered my Beloved's holy service.

Ah, but that was the joy of it! In my youth
I believed what my senses told me. If I couldn't
see taste touch smell or hear it
it didn't exist. I was sure of that. Until God demanded
everything I cherished most: my Beloved's sacred life
my livelihood, my attachment to family friends security
home name country proof everything.

Everything.

I roamed the world and found my faith anew each day
as this family or that shared with me
whatever they had. Some nights I slept in royal chambers;
on others I was lulled to sleep by the whisper of the sea
as I laid my head in the sands of some foreign shore.

> ... *guard him as the pupil of your eye.*

When my time came to leave this mortal body, it was here
on the west coast of India, its southernmost tip,

in the lush and verdant plains of Kerala, that God demanded
my life. And I gave it, most gratefully, surrendering this
perplexing burden—God made human in me.

Every year since, on the anniversary of my death,
they wheel my coffin on its teakwood catafalque
out into the apse of this cathedral.
Thousands of prayerful pilgrims wait
to view my mortal remains, searching
in my miraculously uncorrupt body for a sign
that there is a God; that some Divinity has the power
to answer their prayers.

In this mass of sweating humanity my eye
catches glimpses of illuminati. This woman

in a brown cotton dress, holding her toddler
on her shoulders so the child may breathe

a clearer air; that ancient pushed
along in a makeshift wheelchair

by his rapturous grandson; and there
by the far wall an aging thief

washing his soul clean with tears
of repentance: each of them

bears the glow of inner knowing.
God is everywhere.

Walking up to the coffin, now, is a young man
so jittery, so uneasy in his skin,
that even in the press of this throng
he is set apart. The people near him
pull away, repelled by the aura of violence
he wears around him like a carapace. He edges
nearer the foot of the coffin; bends down,
as others do, brings his mouth to the relic's feet.

Then, sudden screams from the woman behind him
bring the ushers running. There are shrieks and cries
shouts and wailing all around. I look, and see blood
spurting from the right foot of my newly desecrated
body. The young man is kneeling, still, before the coffin
his eyes glazed, unseeing. Tears pour down
his sallow cheeks. The ushers grab him roughly
by his armpits, drag him to his feet. Blood

stains his chin; his mouth is clamped firmly
around the bleeding digit that is my severed big toe.
He has bitten it right off, in a transport of ecstasy
or indignation. And I am angry. This is all that's left
of my incarnation; witness to my terrible struggle with being
human. Now my body, twin and mirror of my Beloved's
own, is utterly defiled, fills the mouth of this hungry
stranger. Like the rumbling of an earthquake, then,

I hear God's loving laughter deep

in my soul: *One more thing, Thomas,
I ask of you. Will you give it? Willingly?* And I struggle
with my heart: "This is all I have left, Lord; why
would you ask this of me?"
God's voice, rutilant with Divine joy: *I do ask it,
Thomas. You are free to say yea or nay. What
will you do?* My soul's answer rises, singing:
"Yes, yes and yes!" even while
this stubborn darkness in me growls, "How can this
be? I am a saint, worthy of reverence. Punish
this man!"

I turn my gaze upon the sacristy. Uniformed
guards come rushing in. They shout questions, exclaim
angrily, wave their arms about. The crowd
presses in. The young man stands meek and amazed,
all the violence drained out of his soul. He says
nothing, bows lower as the voices around him rise
like the tide. The glow of illumination is upon him.
I can see, in his stillness, he hears nothing.
His ears are filled with the voice of God.

And I hear my Beloved's voice, echoing
down the centuries, clear as water now, priceless
gift from this troubled man, my brother,
struggling, as I have done, to reconcile
those fractious twins, human divinity:

> *Love your brother as your soul,
> guard him as the pupil of your eye.*

BODH GAYA

So this is where you sat,
having vowed not to move
until you'd grasped what you were looking for—
the root of human suffering.

To see things as they are. Girders
of life, architecture of light
underlying all creation. You met

demons, temptresses, your own
body's fearful trembling, heartbeat
slipping sideways into a crack of time
no bigger than a sliver, torso held upright
by implacable will. So you sat,
vision turned inward, cross-legged
in the shade of this Bodhi tree. Emerged
at last from your long quest, simooms
blowing through the sockets of your eyes.

Stripped to the bones, this
is what you saw. All phenomena *anicca*—
impermanent as a flower,
death sprouting darkly with the seed.

Sunyata—emptiness—at the heart of all
being. You smiled,
offered a lotus blossom to your faithful disciple
in lieu of a doctrine.

Now, 2400 years later, an adamant temple
towers hundreds of feet into the dusty ochre sky
of Bodh Gaya. Carved with images of your face,
your serene smile repeated over
and over, ubiquitous as the Golden
Arches. Your radical discovery of nothingness
is surrounded now by an economic empire.

Priests, pilgrims, vendors of yak tea
and prayer flags. Rivers of coins empty
into temple coffers. Young Tibetan monks
perform a hundred thousand prostrations
in the cobbled walkway,
kneepads and mittens cushioning the scrape
of shale on flesh. Enlightenment

without *dukkha*. And you smile, oh Buddha,
at these lonely stances on the rim
of the Great Void.

BUDDHIST CHRONICLES

1.

Yashodhara and Siddhartha: the parting

Would you leave me, Siddhartha? This bed,
its crumpled sheets still bear the imprint
of our bodies. Look, I will cut off my hair,
these heavy tresses you love to twine around your wrists;
I will lock my legs around your waist.
I will not let you go.

Will you leave me?

I left my father's orchards for you,
learned to love these echoing hills
because they are your home.
My only home is you.
I left them all: my mother, who wept at our wedding,
like the Ganges in full flood; my father, brother,
the country of my birth.
I came to you bereft of language;
we spoke in whispers of blood, thunder of flesh
rejoicing. Do you remember? We made love
on the balcony until it broke and we fell,
still entwined, onto the ground below.

And now you tell me you must go?

You say you've looked into the entrails
of suffering and cannot rest until you know
how the story ends. Your mind trembled
when you met that unholy trinity:
sickness old age death.
But we are young, Siddhartha,
my belly leaps with new life. Stay.
Stay for your child
if not for me.

Why can you not stay? Does my beauty
unman you? Your mouth flutters like a bird
beneath my fingers and my heart shouts
in my chest and yet, the curve of my lips,
is it the entrance to death's cave?
Must you go?

2.

Rejection

Don't preach to me, Siddhartha. You are an old man
who masquerades in a young man's clothes.
Don't talk to me of afterlife; I know what I know.
My body is my guide. Beat of pulse, belly's cry,
the raging of my thighs tell me all I need to know.
Your heavenly consolations are not for me.

Go to your hermit's cave, Siddhartha. Reject
the body's truths of blood and bone
for arid philosophical perfection.
Sultry night and all the burning stars will
bed with me when you are gone.

3.

Rahula's demand

Where is my father?
Why do you sit all day by the window
gazing out at the sky, and at this winding path
that leads away from our mountain kingdom?

Mother, come, play with me. I have a new monkey
with soft white fur, black rings around his eyes;
he speaks to me in monkey tongue,
tells me stories of the bazaar.

Why must I stay here in grandfather's palace?
It is pestilent with women and old men
hiding from the cold.

I want to see my father.
Take me to him.

4.

Prajapati

I loved Siddhartha as my own
my sister's child, suckled
at my breast

but I saw him always
for what he was

a prince
shielded by garden walls.

He had never known death;
even the flowers in his orchards

were picked before their petals fell.
He never knew the stench of decay

or the rotting fruit
life vomits up.

Yasodhara was different;
she knew their happiness was fragile

a pale blue egg bravely held
in the hollow of her hand.

She fought for it

while he, who had never been denied
crushed it

in his fist.

And yet, he was tender,
an orchid sweetening this mountain air

his father's prize.

He could have turned out spoiled as a peacock
all those palaces built for him, all those

dancing girls with naked breasts and
rubies gleaming in their pubic hair.

But he had a purity of heart that would not let him
sink into these pleasures. He was very young

when his cousin shot a swan and claimed it
as his trophy. Siddhartha drew the arrow from the bird's

bleeding breast, warmed her injured heart against his own,
nursed her till she healed
and flew away.

Still, he was a prince
raised to believe
the kingdom took wing from him.

Selfish in his way, as she in hers, he was all
clarity and air,
cool detachment;

she was earth, and water.

Asceticism.
Appetite.

And yet, they chose each other.

This is the secret that overflows
in her eyes.

I wasn't surprised when he left,
though I feared for Yasodhara's sanity.

5.

Yasodhara's lament

Tides of grief
through my veins

From this swollen heart into estuaries

I mourn the wrack
to come

I have stored pain like marrow
like treasure in the caves

of my bones

Bloodwaters crash and break
on this spiny shore

6.
Suddhodana's dilemma

The king sits in council
with his ministers. His heir
has vanished,
choosing the ascetic's empty bowl
over the imperial crown.

Seven sages predicted this
the day Siddhartha was born.
His would be a destiny of choice:
Emperor
or Enlightened One.

The king tried
to keep his heir at home. He buried
the writhing of the flesh
under garments of gold.
Ascetics were plentiful as leaves.
He had only one first-born son.

Now he wrinkles the imperial forehead.
Turns brusquely to his chief minister,
orders Prince Nanda to be brought
to the council chamber.

7.

Siddhartha at the boundary of the Sakya kingdom

Moonless night; cloud
silk across lowering sky.

In my father's palace Yasodhara sleeps,
my son's newborn body curled against her breast:
a snail in its shell.

I have turned my trembling back
on all I love,

tethered still by ropes of desire,
longing. O heart

that hammers against the doors of the sky—
I creep forward to meet this cryptic night.

The river hisses, a cobra at my feet.
I can bear no more goodbyes.

I must make a fist of this heart.

Channa, take my clothes;
these silks and jewels chafe like a yoke.

Give them to my father. Tell him, I will return

when I have found the jewel I seek. Kanthaka,
you must gallop back to the palace too.

I cannot take you with me.

8.
At the boundary: the river Anoma

You stand on my northern bank,
a lacerated young man, with tender-soled feet.
Your tears prick my skin;
droplets of salt swirl in secret eddies.

Do you know what you invoke, O prince?
I am as wide as the chasm between lives.
My waters erase the known world.
My ways are ancient
and hard. I dwindle mountains into pebbles
round and smooth as pearls.
There is no immunity here.
Men have drowned in these currents.

You hack off your hair with a sword, leave it blowing
like straw on my flanks. But that which you sever
once you step into my belly
will bleed dark as rubies:
fearful, benevolent as death itself.

Loneliness will wear you down with the slow grinding
of millstones. Your mind will be drenched in fear
and hunger. You will twist in currents of longing
while fish nibble at your entrails.

Think well, before you enter my embrace.

9.

Yasodhara

Yesterday
the magnolia's perfect bowl
brimmed with rain-water

Now, a single petal,
mottled cream and brown,
droops outward

The bowl is broken

Rahula runs towards me
his laughing face upturned

Two raindrops tremble
on the blossom's ivory lip

YOU

Your blessings have flowed down
like rain upon these pages

Your voice in my throat, your words
from my fingertips

You take my stubborn smallness
and stretch me into eternity

You the ruby blood that
surges in my heart

You, Beloved, you

PEACE RISES

The sea draws a pewter veil
across her shining

and dawn's pomegranate smile
feathers to grey

Even the clouds hold their breath as
Peace rises from her

winter grave, belly brimming
with hidden light

ACKNOWLEDGEMENTS

A heart full of gratitude for my sons, Jesse and James, and my grand-daughter, Kaedance. Thank you for your love, beauty, kindness and joy.

Thanks to poets and editors George McWhirter, Priscilla Uppal, and Ron Smith, who helped shaped previous versions of some of these poems.

Thanks to Mansfield Press and Oolichan Books for publishing earlier versions of some of these poems.

Thanks to my incomparable designer, Richard Miller, who builds beautiful homes for my words with his art, and who designed both the interior and cover of this book.

Thanks to Mandy McIlwraith and Helen Hunter MacKenzie, who do the essential work to bring this book to life and into your hands.

Thank you to Judith Snider, for a lifetime of friendship and unwavering love and support.

Gratitude beyond words to the poets whose art is beacon, inspiration, home and belonging for me. Your names are too many to list, but you, and your words, live in me.

Thank you to each of you who read my books and make a home for them on your bookshelves and in your hearts.

HIRO BOGA is an award-winning writer, business strategist, mentor, teacher, and founder of the Deva Alchemy Academy. She is the author of five books, most recently *To Be Soul, Do Soul: Adventures in Creative Consciousness*. She was born and raised in India, and lives and works on the west coast of Canada.

hiroboga.com

www.ingramcontent.com/pod-product-compliance
Lightning Source LLC
Chambersburg PA
CBHW022042200426
43209CB00072B/1925/J